This book belongs to

_____

RECIPES	STARTERS	SOUPS	MAIN DISHES	SIDE DISHES	DESSERTS	DRINKS			
1									
2									
3									
4									
5									
6									
7									
8									
9									
10									
11									
12									
13									
14									
15									
16									
17									
18									
19									
20									
21									
22									
23									
24									
25									

RECIPES	STARTERS	SOUPS	MAIN DISHES	SIDE DISHES	DESSERTS	DRINKS			
26									
27									
28									
29									
30									
31									
32									
33									
34									
35									
36									
37									
38									
39									
40									
41									
42									
43									
44									
45									
46									
47									
48									
49									
50									

RECIPES	STARTERS	SOUPS	MAIN DISHES	SIDE DISHES	DESSERTS	DRINKS			
51									
52									
53									
54									
55									
56									
57									
58									
59									
60									
61									
62									
63									
64									
65									
66									
67									
68									
69									
70									
71									
72									
73									
74									
75									

RECIPES	STARTERS	SOUPS	MAIN DISHES	SIDE DISHES	DESSERTS	DRINKS			
76									
77									
78									
79									
80									
81									
82									
83									
84									
85									
86									
87									
88									
89									
90									
91									
92									
93									
94									
95									
96									
97									
98									
99									
100									

RECIPE

1

TIME:
SERVES:
DIFFICULTY:

INGREDIENTS

METHOD

RECIPE

TIME:
SERVES:
DIFFICULTY:

INGREDIENTS

METHOD

RECIPE

TIME:
SERVES:
DIFFICULTY:

INGREDIENTS

METHOD

RECIPE

TIME:
SERVES:
DIFFICULTY:

INGREDIENTS

METHOD

RECIPE

TIME:
SERVES:
DIFFICULTY:

INGREDIENTS

METHOD

RECIPE

TIME:
SERVES:
DIFFICULTY:

INGREDIENTS

METHOD

RECIPE

⑦

TIME:
SERVES:
DIFFICULTY:

INGREDIENTS

METHOD

RECIPE

TIME:
SERVES:
DIFFICULTY:

INGREDIENTS

METHOD

RECIPE

TIME:
SERVES:
DIFFICULTY:

INGREDIENTS

METHOD

RECIPE

TIME:
SERVES:
DIFFICULTY:

INGREDIENTS

METHOD

RECIPE

11

TIME:
SERVES:
DIFFICULTY:

INGREDIENTS

METHOD

RECIPE

TIME:
SERVES:
DIFFICULTY:

INGREDIENTS

METHOD

RECIPE

TIME:
SERVES:
DIFFICULTY:

INGREDIENTS

METHOD

RECIPE

TIME:
SERVES:
DIFFICULTY:

INGREDIENTS

METHOD

RECIPE

TIME:
SERVES:
DIFFICULTY:

INGREDIENTS

METHOD

RECIPE

TIME:
SERVES:
DIFFICULTY:

INGREDIENTS

METHOD

RECIPE

(17)

TIME:
SERVES:
DIFFICULTY:

INGREDIENTS

METHOD

RECIPE

TIME:
SERVES:
DIFFICULTY:

INGREDIENTS

METHOD

RECIPE

TIME:
SERVES:
DIFFICULTY:

INGREDIENTS

METHOD

RECIPE

TIME:
SERVES:
DIFFICULTY:

INGREDIENTS

METHOD

RECIPE

TIME:
SERVES:
DIFFICULTY:

INGREDIENTS

METHOD

RECIPE

TIME:
SERVES:
DIFFICULTY:

INGREDIENTS

METHOD

RECIPE

TIME:
SERVES:
DIFFICULTY:

INGREDIENTS

METHOD

RECIPE

TIME:
SERVES:
DIFFICULTY:

INGREDIENTS

METHOD

RECIPE

TIME:
SERVES:
DIFFICULTY:

INGREDIENTS

METHOD

RECIPE

TIME:
SERVES:
DIFFICULTY:

INGREDIENTS

METHOD

RECIPE

TIME:
SERVES:
DIFFICULTY:

INGREDIENTS

METHOD

RECIPE

TIME:
SERVES:
DIFFICULTY:

INGREDIENTS

METHOD

RECIPE

TIME:
SERVES:
DIFFICULTY:

INGREDIENTS

METHOD

RECIPE

TIME:
SERVES:
DIFFICULTY:

INGREDIENTS

METHOD

RECIPE

TIME:
SERVES:
DIFFICULTY:

INGREDIENTS

METHOD

RECIPE

TIME:
SERVES:
DIFFICULTY:

INGREDIENTS

METHOD

RECIPE

TIME:
SERVES:
DIFFICULTY:

INGREDIENTS

METHOD

RECIPE

TIME:
SERVES:
DIFFICULTY:

INGREDIENTS

METHOD

RECIPE

TIME:
SERVES:
DIFFICULTY:

INGREDIENTS

METHOD

RECIPE

TIME:
SERVES:
DIFFICULTY:

INGREDIENTS

METHOD

RECIPE

TIME:
SERVES:
DIFFICULTY:

INGREDIENTS

METHOD

RECIPE

TIME:
SERVES:
DIFFICULTY:

INGREDIENTS

METHOD

RECIPE

TIME:
SERVES:
DIFFICULTY:

INGREDIENTS

METHOD

RECIPE

TIME:
SERVES:
DIFFICULTY:

INGREDIENTS

METHOD

RECIPE

(41)

TIME:
SERVES:
DIFFICULTY:

INGREDIENTS

METHOD

RECIPE

TIME:
SERVES:
DIFFICULTY:

INGREDIENTS

METHOD

RECIPE

TIME:
SERVES:
DIFFICULTY:

INGREDIENTS

METHOD

RECIPE

TIME:
SERVES:
DIFFICULTY:

INGREDIENTS

METHOD

RECIPE

TIME:
SERVES:
DIFFICULTY:

INGREDIENTS

METHOD

RECIPE

TIME:
SERVES:
DIFFICULTY:

INGREDIENTS

METHOD

RECIPE

TIME:
SERVES:
DIFFICULTY:

INGREDIENTS

METHOD

RECIPE

TIME:
SERVES:
DIFFICULTY:

INGREDIENTS

METHOD

RECIPE

49

TIME:
SERVES:
DIFFICULTY:

INGREDIENTS

METHOD

RECIPE

TIME:
SERVES:
DIFFICULTY:

INGREDIENTS

METHOD

RECIPE

(51)

TIME:
SERVES:
DIFFICULTY:

INGREDIENTS

METHOD

RECIPE

TIME:
SERVES:
DIFFICULTY:

INGREDIENTS

METHOD

RECIPE

TIME:
SERVES:
DIFFICULTY:

INGREDIENTS

METHOD

RECIPE

TIME:
SERVES:
DIFFICULTY:

INGREDIENTS

METHOD

RECIPE

TIME:
SERVES:
DIFFICULTY:

INGREDIENTS

METHOD

RECIPE

TIME:
SERVES:
DIFFICULTY:

INGREDIENTS

METHOD

RECIPE

57

TIME:
SERVES:
DIFFICULTY:

INGREDIENTS

METHOD

RECIPE

TIME:
SERVES:
DIFFICULTY:

INGREDIENTS

METHOD

RECIPE

TIME:
SERVES:
DIFFICULTY:

INGREDIENTS

METHOD

RECIPE

TIME:
SERVES:
DIFFICULTY:

INGREDIENTS

METHOD

RECIPE

TIME:
SERVES:
DIFFICULTY:

INGREDIENTS

METHOD

RECIPE

TIME:
SERVES:
DIFFICULTY:

INGREDIENTS

METHOD

RECIPE

TIME:
SERVES:
DIFFICULTY:

INGREDIENTS

METHOD

RECIPE

TIME:
SERVES:
DIFFICULTY:

INGREDIENTS

METHOD

RECIPE

TIME:
SERVES:
DIFFICULTY:

INGREDIENTS

METHOD

RECIPE

TIME:
SERVES:
DIFFICULTY:

INGREDIENTS

METHOD

RECIPE

TIME:
SERVES:
DIFFICULTY:

INGREDIENTS

METHOD

RECIPE

TIME:
SERVES:
DIFFICULTY:

INGREDIENTS

METHOD

RECIPE

TIME:
SERVES:
DIFFICULTY:

INGREDIENTS

METHOD

// RECIPE

TIME:
SERVES:
DIFFICULTY:

INGREDIENTS

METHOD

RECIPE

(71)

TIME:
SERVES:
DIFFICULTY:

INGREDIENTS

METHOD

RECIPE

TIME:
SERVES:
DIFFICULTY:

INGREDIENTS

METHOD

RECIPE

TIME:
SERVES:
DIFFICULTY:

INGREDIENTS

METHOD

RECIPE

TIME:
SERVES:
DIFFICULTY:

INGREDIENTS

METHOD

RECIPE

TIME:
SERVES:
DIFFICULTY:

INGREDIENTS

METHOD

RECIPE

TIME:
SERVES:
DIFFICULTY:

INGREDIENTS

METHOD

RECIPE

TIME:
SERVES:
DIFFICULTY:

INGREDIENTS

METHOD

RECIPE

TIME:
SERVES:
DIFFICULTY:

INGREDIENTS

METHOD

RECIPE

TIME:
SERVES:
DIFFICULTY:

INGREDIENTS

METHOD

RECIPE

TIME:
SERVES:
DIFFICULTY:

INGREDIENTS

METHOD

RECIPE

TIME:
SERVES:
DIFFICULTY:

INGREDIENTS

METHOD

RECIPE

TIME:
SERVES:
DIFFICULTY:

INGREDIENTS

METHOD

RECIPE

TIME:
SERVES:
DIFFICULTY:

INGREDIENTS

METHOD

RECIPE

TIME:
SERVES:
DIFFICULTY:

INGREDIENTS

METHOD

RECIPE

TIME:
SERVES:
DIFFICULTY:

INGREDIENTS

METHOD

RECIPE

_____

TIME:
SERVES:
DIFFICULTY:

INGREDIENTS

_____   _____
_____   _____
_____   _____
_____   _____
_____   _____

METHOD

_____
_____
_____
_____
_____
_____
_____
_____

RECIPE

TIME:
SERVES:
DIFFICULTY:

INGREDIENTS

METHOD

RECIPE

_____

TIME:
SERVES:
DIFFICULTY:

INGREDIENTS

METHOD

RECIPE

TIME:
SERVES:
DIFFICULTY:

INGREDIENTS

METHOD

RECIPE

TIME:
SERVES:
DIFFICULTY:

INGREDIENTS

METHOD

RECIPE

TIME:
SERVES:
DIFFICULTY:

INGREDIENTS

METHOD

RECIPE

TIME:
SERVES:
DIFFICULTY:

INGREDIENTS

METHOD

RECIPE

TIME:
SERVES:
DIFFICULTY:

INGREDIENTS

METHOD

RECIPE

TIME:
SERVES:
DIFFICULTY:

INGREDIENTS

METHOD

RECIPE

TIME:
SERVES:
DIFFICULTY:

INGREDIENTS

METHOD

RECIPE

TIME:
SERVES:
DIFFICULTY:

INGREDIENTS

METHOD

RECIPE

_____

TIME:
SERVES:
DIFFICULTY:

INGREDIENTS

METHOD

RECIPE

TIME:
SERVES:
DIFFICULTY:

INGREDIENTS

METHOD

RECIPE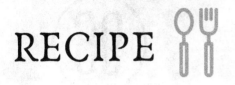

TIME:
SERVES:
DIFFICULTY:

INGREDIENTS

METHOD

RECIPE

TIME:
SERVES:
DIFFICULTY:

INGREDIENTS

METHOD

NOTES

NOTES

NOTES

NOTES

NOTES

NOTES

NOTES

NOTES

NOTES

NOTES

NOTES

NOTES

NOTES

NOTES

NOTES

Printed in the USA
CPSIA information can be obtained
at www.ICGtesting.com
LVHW051606051224
798429LV00011B/486